Othello in the Pyramid of Dreams

OTHELLO IN THE PYRAMID OF DREAMS

AND OTHER POEMS

DONALD ATKINSON

1996

To the Bright Lady

Published by Arc Publications
Nanholme Mill, Shaw Wood Road
Todmorden, Lancs. OL14 6DA

Design Tony Ward
Printed by Arc & Throstle Press
Nanholme Mill, Todmorden, Lancs.

ISBN 1 900072 02 5

Acknowledgements:
Some of the poems in this collection have been published in various poetry magazines and anthologies. 'Brother Ass' and 'Exequy' in *Lines Review* (1994); 'The Child's Play of Antichrist' and parts 2 and 3 of 'Food for the gods' in *Stand*; and 'Punctum', 'Closure' and 'Maggiolate' in *Ambit*. 'Othello in the Pyramid of Dreams' appeared in Issues 4 & 5 of *Sheffield Thursday* (Sheffield Hallam University (1994). 'The arithmetician and his mother' from this sequence also appeared in the British Council anthology *New Writing 5*

The publishers acknowledge financial assistance from Yorkshire and Humberside Arts Board.

Contents

PART I: OTHELLO IN THE PYRAMID OF DREAMS
1. Barefoot to Palestine: Emilia / 9
2. Iago in Egypt / 12
3. The arithmetician and his mother: Michael Cassio / 14
4. Self-portrait in a black mirror: Othello / 15
5. Dreams from the book of the dead / 16
6. Burial / 26
7. Afterworld / 29
8. Sati / 37

PART II:
Mene, mene . . . / 41
The Child's Play of Antichrist / 43
Food for the gods: a triptych from the Iliad
1. los machos / 46
2. la pena / 48
3. funeral games / 49
An invasion of privacy / 52
Punctum / 54
Closure / 56
Exequy / 58
In waterlight / 60
Brother Ass / 62
Maggiolaté / 63

Author's Note

After an introductory quartet, to establish the base of the pyramid squarely in Shakespeare's play, the poem presents a downward journey into the psychic roots of male insecurity, followed by an upward transformation from the psychic to the spiritual. The voices of the traveller and his feminine psychopomp derive from the characters of Othello and Desdemona. However, inasmuch as their journey takes place within the imagined 'pyramid' of the title, they gradually shift shape into the shades of Isis and Osiris.

The pyramid has two aspects: first an underworld of psychological binding and sepulture; and then the afterworld of the circumpolar stars, with the spirit-paths which lead to it. The imagery of ancient Egyptian burial rites is by now almost too well known to need explanation. However, a richly detailed account is given by Christiane Desroches-Noblecourt in *Tutankhamen* (Penguin 1972). More recently, Robert Bauval and Adrian Gilbert have argued a direct connection between the layout of the pyramids at Giza, and the star-map of the heavens at the time when they were built (*The Orion Mystery*, Heinemann 1994; and two features on television). Their research suggests that the purpose of earlier funeral ceremonies was to project into the heavens the buried king Osiris, by means of a coital union with his consort Isis when she rose in the night sky as the Dog Star, Sirius. This union was believed to take place in a chamber of the Great Pyramid, via a narrow shaft which served as a spirit-path. One such shaft was recently explored with a miniaturised camera, to reveal the tiny door of a hitherto unsuspected secret chamber.

All this has contributed to the imagery and narrative of the poem, and to its underlying theme: a psychic return-to-source, and the complementary process of healing. Bearing in mind that of all Shakespeare's central characters, Othello and Leontes are these days the least susceptible to audience-identification, and the most subject to what in therapy counts as 'denial', this might be still a necessary journey.

I

Othello in the Pyramid of Dreams

An aftermath in borrowed voices

1

Barefoot to Palestine: Emilia

So come my soul to bliss as I speak true;
So speaking as I think, I die, I die.
Shakespeare's *Othello*, Act V ii 249

My husband was right, of course: I had them both,
Cassio *and* his General. But not the general camp.
I draw the line at men from underground.
So? He deserved promotion; and at the time
this seemed the quickest way. Not that it worked,
mind you. But all wrapped up and laid to rest
a while before he got involved with her.
And no: it wasn't what you're thinking,
the act itself. We shouldn't talk like that,
or expect so much; they're bound to disappoint.
But it was all right. And I have to admit,
a lot better than what I was used to.
Thick-lips my husband called him. He could have done
with some of that. Like kissing a tortoise.

And Cassio? Our little arithmetician?
I made a meal of him. Partly for sport,
and partly led to compensate myself
for Lodovico's never-never lip.
Not such a bad second-best, the Lieutenant.
And you won't deny he's good-looking?
Which helped make up for limitations
in other departments.
And now you see why he flirted so openly
with *her*: to put my husband off the scent.
That didn't work either. He had a nose
could sniff out smegma in a Carmelite.
He'd sit up in bed, like one of the Three Bears.
So! Who's been screwing in MY nightcap?
Every time the same. And then he'd take me
(when I let him) from behind; for all the world
as if I were a boy, and he Lord Jupiter.
It wasn't women he wanted, really;

but some obscure revenge on men.
I lay with Cassio lately. Fat chance of that!

Why did I marry him? Well, I enjoy
travel; and being a mercenary's wife
you get plenty. You meet attractive men.
And I had ambitions, in which the appointment
to my lady's service played a part.
As for the sexual side – that sort of thing
no-one finds out until too late, don't you agree?

And now, I'm told, they've made a hero of him
in the modern style. Apparently,
the men all cheer him and the women drool.
I don't know what they see in him, the shit.
It's down to the directors, I suppose.
And they're mostly men; reluctant to admit
how prone they are to the same viruses
that rot my husband. No accolades
for coming out about those! But plenty
for telling lies and spreading the disease.

As for her death: I hold myself
as much responsible as anyone.
I ought to have seen what he was up to.
Perhaps I did, not wanting to know,
and fearful of discovery. *Handkerchiefs*!
He had a thing about them. Lord only knows
why such a dry hand needed so many.
I do feel bad about that, I will confess.
But worse was when she looked at me and said:
Dost thou in conscience think, tell me Emilia,
that there be women do abuse their husbands
in such gross kind? I coped, made a handsome speech,
but knew she'd seen the hot flush at my throat
and covered for me. As she did for him
in miraculous words: *Nobody*; *I myself*;
farewell. Commend me to my kind lord.

I've always been one for equality.
If you court more women, I'll sleep with more men
sounds a fair bargain; and for most of us

the best that we can get. Nobody's perfect.
Yet what she said, across those folded sheets,
made me think for a moment there might be
a better way of dealing with it.
Jealousy (ours and theirs) is what I mean.
But that would involve a journey; barefoot,
bare-souled. And far further than Palestine.
Before death or after, am I up to it?

I sit here, on the steps of this pyramid,
watching a column of ants crawl from the tomb.
Inside, some buried king embalms himself.
Othello's type. And lumbered with my husband.

2

Iago in Egypt

In the Great Pyramid of Khufu at Giza, archaeologists have uncovered a sloping shaft, eight inches square, which leads to a secret chamber, as yet unopened. The shaft is believed to have served as a spirit-path to and from the stars, in the after-life of buried kings.

Tomb-robbing Ancient, breathing hard,
I yield my twenty grammes of dew
to these sluggish air-currents,
here where the pale gums of time
eat at a womb's lining.
It will all come away with the birth.

Small and square as the dark hole
of a cat-flap, the spirit-path slopes up
at forty-five degrees. To gain
the eventual door, I make like
shrunk Alice. My fingers, grasping
the copper handles, are a child's.

And it won't shift. I scrape a nail
down the gap between wall and door.
This filtering of fine black dust
the decayed swaddling-clothes of parents.
Make me a jarring atomy
among these motes, and fibre-optic!

I'm in. They shacked up here then
(the silver bones of my father,
the gold skin of my mother)
not in the *Royal Chambers* mis-named,
the flesh turned to beeswax, the hair
gone flaxen as night-linen.

Two senile foetuses, they lie
on beds of bulrush side by side,
vulva and phallus sealed
in the warm green woody scent of chypre.

Horus the falcon builds his nest
in each dark fold of the swaddling.

Your hero in the black jaundice,
I am indeed a camera
and mean to catch the moment.
Black is the colour of rebirth.
My two eyes rhinestones in soot,
I engross the divine shadow.

In the obsidian of my soul
I record my own begetting.
Beast-with-two-backs, they're at it now.
When I run the tape, I am not what I am.

Like forty thieves
I move among these twenty-two black jars
crammed with alternatives: my brother's chromosomes.
I love them all! I long to break the seals,
and in the lucky draw try on
his *more expressive lip*, that straighter nose;
see how I look with eyes less pigging small,
shoulders not quite so rounded (bigger cock of course)
and whiter teeth. Then have the women crawl.

Why can't they get it right, the pair of them:
make us *both* handsome; use quality-control?
God damn them for this muzzle, bent as a crooked back –
small chance for usurpers in the kingdom of the genes!
What can I lose? I'll crack the code,
plunge like the whale-hunting cherubim
up to the elbows in sperm AND SQUEEZE IT!
We'll make the pips of nature's germens squeak.
I'll have you by the tail, my handsome brother.
Oh *you'll be bored* with penetration now.
Think of it as a game of dressing-up:
I'll wear your beauty like a scented sheath,
and give you – my diseases!

3

The arithmetician and his mother: Michael Cassio

In the field that runs by the Roman aqueduct
I trot beside her. Folds of her summer dress
make a bunch of flowers in my fist; and the grass
so deep, it wets my knees with cuckoo-spit.
Little frog-hopper, all of a lather,
I can hop too, and skip, and fall about
in this apocalyptic green; till she laughs
and I think she likes me, do it all again,
could keep this up until the cows come home.
Until in truth, like something prophesied, they do,
across the bottom of the field lugubriously.

A blotchy one lags far behind the rest.

Suddenly grown finger-wise, we count the cows.
And then we count the blotches on the cow.
Over and over; each time a different tally.

Have I ever known anything for sure?
Did I live in her eye, her airy pupil,
or was there another? Collapse of the wave-
function at the point of measurement,
sway of the universe. How hold them together,
the blotches and the counting and the cow?
Why is there so much light tonight,
has she merged with the planet Jupiter?
Who beckons me, who waits for me;
what formulae are written in these stars?

4

Self-portrait in a black mirror: Othello

I chart an unchanging fall of shadow
round these walls. There is no other place
and I have always been here. Though judgement
lights me inside like Acid, I am blind
to the visible world, which swaddles me
in a black skin all over. The eye-holes
look inward; tapers burn in the sockets.
Sure, I had eyes once; but they corrupted.
My skull's a cockpit without audience
or performers now, the last adhesions
of the brain dissolved in those night-sugars.
When they take out the thoughts, they scour the place
with crushed myrrh and cassia. There are echoes still.
Not all the voices are my own.

A hollow death's-head, oiled with candlelight,
I point you down that passage, to the *Gallery*.
You'll find a journey mirrored on its walls.
Our eyes are the longships of the soul.
At a world's end mine spun on their keels twice
and went down. The descent will show you the hour.
Would you know error virtually real,
yet come through to a perilous joy at last?
Then let me mark your forehead with this dust;
white dust from the road, she threw on herself
as she followed me into darkness a little way.
The trace of it still clings, where her white arms held me
against rejection. Moist it with spittle
and seal up your eyes to inward optics.

5

Dreams from the book of the dead

In a circle of sand, crouched in his fringed night-shirt,
fondling the sacred quill between his paws,
not daring to write,
I saw Anubis the dog-child
and knew him for myself.
I felt the urethral chill between his legs
just where he will be eaten
and the teeth that burned on the darkness
like electrodes.

Around me barking and yelping
and screams to set mothers running,
from the conies and squirrels
the mice and small deer pierced with arrows
or harried by wolves with great yellow teeth.
The brush of their fur on my haunches
left blood on my thighs.
But there came a worse sound from behind.

I turned, clutching my shirt-tails, and saw them:
the twelve man-faced baboons in a circle
and she in the midst, dancing,
her clothes coming off
as she handed each one with that smile of hers
setting her lips to their cinnamon-haired fingers.
And when she passed on, each one taking her
there from behind, the quick salamander *I saw it go in*
and felt her flesh quiver. While on to the next.

Till the king of the troupe faced her.
She leapt to him then
her feet in the small of his back
her hair falling away
on her face the familiar rapture
personal once
anonymous now.

And the rest jackal-headed dog-mouthed,
biting and licking her tail from below.
While I, goosed in a night-shirt, looked on,
excluded, affrighted, complicit,
the pain like a voltage
shot through the base of the spine,
the head flooding with acid,
the loss of the self.

Till I howled for admission at last
and they tore me,
the dark flesh glowing like embers.

*

Her breasts of silk, pieced from the self-same skin
        (I touch myself and feel her)
Subdued my father's eye before that sin:
        I sucked her milk to steal her.

He bore a charm to ravish maidens' hearts.
        This hallowed worm displaced him.
She opened to me all her secret parts;
        Reluctantly embraced him.

Mandrake and cornflowers garlanding her hips
        Left me too soon unwise.
The love-fruit of her flesh under my lips;
        Loathed in my father's eyes.

I dream him slowly taking off his coat
        And turning in the mirror.
I see the knife-blade fretting at her throat,
        And in his eyes the terror.

Playing the Cassio to my mother once,
        I learned 'women are frail.'
There needs no Iago. Only a father's mad glance
        Prophesying betrayal.

*

In a far corner
of the *King's Chamber* mis-named
a pillar of feldspar
on a layer of fine sand.

Dagger of flesh
that grew in my side
till the priests cut it away
to be embalmed.

Then swathed in twenty yards
of bandaging,
replaced erect between my legs
and worshipped.

They told me it was everything,
stuffed proud as a goose-neck
in the seven years of plenty
among fat kine.

Then what should poor Thick-lips do
but go for a soldier?
Offering the fore-foot and heart
of a bull.

*

He lay sprinkled like wheat
On the floor of the tomb.
My hands filled with tears
I watered the corn-grains.

In the blood-caves of my womb
The seed came like milk.
He is born
Clothed in a red towel.

Curled on his thigh
Like a birth-mark
A thread from the loom
Of my most secret hair.

Singing
I weave from it
The handkerchief
That tapestries his doom.

*

I smell WREN! he hissed,
pulling at my lapel
and chin-to-chin butting his phizzog,
talking through his teeth.
I said *Where*?
while over his shoulder
I watched her come down the steps
in that uniform:
dusk of her black-stockinged thighs
inside her skirt,
under that Navy serge
the tight-houseled bum
sidling.
And all the time over his shoulder
she's coming towards us.
I tell you, he says, gritting:
I can smell DOG!

Then she stands right behind him
and kisses me over his shoulder.
He whips round,
and we're both slapping her face
but *so fast* it's like hyperventilating.
When she drops to her knees gasping and pleading
we don't stop
and I know what will happen next,
but right now there's a crack in my brain
and it's *him*, with this long needle
in at my side like a rapier
Rapier? *Rape yer*!
Goes in like a needle
cuts like a blade.

Till I fall,
a wasp sliced in two,
and catch sight of her face
screaming over his shoulder.

*

From his bed strewn with jasmine
I raised myself up,
Setting aside the pillow
And laying by the sheets.

O viscera, viscera,
These men, these men.

He fetched a silk napkin
And tied up my head,
Pressing down the pillow
And binding close the sheets.

The fault is in their eyes,
Not in our stars.

As we lay among wild lupins
I handed him the cup,
The living gold so yellow
And the thorned rose so sweet.

At him, at him alone.
How came the light broken?

Black was the love-making
White was the sheet,
When they fetched out his bowels
And embalmed his feet.

We go bare-soled to Palestine,
Seeking the cause, the cause.

*

It's a play-room,
with toys all round the skirting.
In a triangle of vision
we crouch on hair-cord carpet
childhood troilists.

It seems she has only one breast
between us two
and I have missed my turn.

I call out to her:
Look at me!
But instead
she leans across
and touches his thigh
repeatedly.

He laughs,
she smiles.
Her nipple is an eye
with milk for tears.

There's failure at my heart,
strength gone from knees and fingers
on the rock-face.
Worse: as I'm falling
it's he who catches me,
touches me there.

Forsaken brother
rival
Smenkharē,
your arms are crushing me,
I'm blacked out in your kiss.

Fearing that most
which I refuse to embrace
each night I dream about you.

We wrestle of course.
And predictably
when I wake shouting
my thigh is out of joint.

*

I clothe myself in the blue-white milk of the sky.
        In one of those same sheets.
        Shroud me in one of those same sheets.

My maids from the four winds lifted it over my head.
        It hung round me like clouds.
        It hung round me in long white clouds.

Seven priests went before; they bore pitchers brimming
                                        with milk.
        And poured it on the ground.
        And poured it out upon the dry ground.

My husband is blind; an ignorant still-born child.
        I shall wash him in milk.
        I shall wash him live with my milk.

My milk is white as hailstones; it will itch his eye.
        We bathe his hands and feet.
        We bathe his wrinkled hands and feet.

*

Taking a stone of Ethiopia,
the iron adze, seeded from meteorite,
and with its sharp edge striking himself,
he made a corridor
for that uncircumcisèd dog his heart
to bark at moonbeams.
Thrusting a hand deep under the rib
he groped as if for pearls; but found instead
this fleshy oyster, cowrie-shaped and warm,
which kissed his finger with an inside lip
and sucked and sucked.
Then tore it out, and dashed it on the ground.
And while he watched, it turned into a toad;
pulsing, jewel-headed, in the chamber corner.

*

In the marshes of Chemnis
the village girls
who know they will be raped
hide razor-blades in their vaginas.
Watch the soldiers bleed to death
or worse.

So Agamemnon died,
finding her in the bath
her legs apart.
No axe
and no Aegisthus.

Orestes in every woman all his life will flee
that darkening thicket where the shark-teeth wait.

Son: act the mother-fucker now; come on.
You play the bull. I'll be your cow.

*

They are dancing the death of the heart
        In a necklace of mandrakes
        A gorget of cornflowers
With scented cones on their heads.

It runs down their faces like nard.
        It drips from their dreadlocks
        The tips of their fingers.
The oils of embalming are black.

Beating the side-drum of Shiva's
        Left hand and left eye
        They garland a foetus
In chaplets of eggs from the toad.

Hathor the Goddess my Mother is drunk.
        Her seven hanging dolls
        Are lifting their skirts.
They are dancing me into her womb.

She is hoist on the grave-bed of Tueris.
        The chaplet of cornflowers
        The garland of mandrakes
Fall from her hips and her shoulders.

Aeropé, a moon on each flank
        Is the Goddess my Mother.
        Or salt Cleopatra, tail in the air
As bound I am carried to meet her.

In the swamps of the delta, Anubis the dog-child
        Rocks in his caul on a bed of papyrus
        Sealed in a cradle of bulrushes
Horus the falcon.

I am plough, I am coulter, I share her.
        I sail between her moons.
        I find in her all these wet mouths
And seed my pearls in them like teeth.

I drown, I am grain of wheat in the flood.
        I go down, down,
        Among the earth-lips, the clyster-pipes,
A film of husk, that clings around a seed.

This is the final sojourn in the Abyss, the death of the heart.
        No face, no likeness here.
        Yet something fades I lost.
Shadows *like her .. or like her .. or like her who* ...
                                        disappear.

*

He who hides the hours
inscribes the sentence:

seventy days
nine months and a half
or sixteen years.

Time
times
and half a time.

Life.

Scratches of a bird's beak
on the granite wall.

Thoth: the Arbiter.

*

6

Burial

Nosing through papery reeds that cut the wrist
we shaped up-river in a blue canoe,
the god lying bandaged amidships.
There dwell the anthropophagi, and men
with one huge foot, that shades them when they sleep.
Canopus was our guide, who took as fare
the cuckold Menelaus in his search
for Helen of the Trees – another story.
He stood in the bows, and brandished the harpoon.
We worked with boomerang, which fly to the hand
like answering peregrines. Along the bank
the god's tame cheetah, weeping purple tears
roamed a masterless hound, savaging
all hostile beasts that came too near. Ibex
are dangerous, and certain fish are evil.
Worse are the noisome wildfowl; worst of all
the hurt abomination that they guard.
The lad Ihy kept them off as best he could
working the far shore with his band of ephebes
jingling away with the sistra, dancing about.
Some of those girls he has in tow have nice legs.
Perhaps on the way back, we told ourselves.

And how were we to know? We paddled on
through bloodied waters, nursing our dead freight.
The air grew thick with feathers; carcases
thumped on the thwarts, heaving up shattered wings.
None of us dared touch, but let them lie,
mingling our hard-fought breathing with their last –
the vermin. And so upstream for seventy days.
Exhausted, unprepared, we turned the last slow bend,
and there it rose: the abominable cave
huge as a whole mountain, opening
to engulf us; the appalled and wounded Eye
from which the turbid river flowed against us

like the infected mucus from a stye.
Here was the stabbed iris of that Underworld
which aye with weeping stinks and stinking weeps
and sorrows for its wound eternally.
We drew our boat toward the nether lid
and hung there on the lasher. Four of us
lifted the swaddled body in the air
and tossed it forward, where it fell to dark.
Then shipped our paddles, swung round with the stream,
and slept the miles we'd come the other way.
Somewhere on that dream journey down-river
we thought we heard girls' voices calling to us, singing;
but were too weak by then to lift our heads.

*

O viscera, viscera,
this man, this man.

See where his inwards are parted.
My sisters from the four winds
have drawn out the brain through the nostrils
have lifted the wings of his breathing
have pulled up desire by the roots
and laid them in store.
How shall they save them from the forty thieves?

*

Sure my imaginations were unclean.
Adrift on a sea of undoing,
they fouled up long ago in Vulcan's stithy.
When the diseased eye complies with its own worm
even rational daylight breeds monsters.
The essential self's astray, deceived, bereft,
looking for one with whom you're holding hands.
I knew what *I* was; not what *she* should be.

Naught to do now but learn that I am dead.
Repentance is a type of florid nausea,
I feed on the taste of waterbrash.

The horns of the three great ventricles are void,
death-angels hover there. Their wings infold
with these lines, this blank verse, someone sets down.

*

In the mind's green eye
in a circle of still water
the spirit-boat is centred:
becalmed among monsters.

*

7

Afterworld

*

Where his body on the waters
floated in pieces, a torn sonnet,
she in love's night fishing caught him
as they net the flying gar-fish in the Southern seas,
startling by torchlight.

At the water's edge
I saw a fire of coals,
with parts of a man's body
heaped up like loaves.
And the Woman kneeling,
a thread between her teeth,
stitching the broken morsels
with bites of love.

The fragments that remain.

As on a loom
rocking the flayed body between her legs,
she weaves a skein of sex
to clothe him in.
He wakes in the mesh of love.

The lips and the skin remember like the soul.

Her kisses glass him to crystal.
Clear as *ginèvre*
the blood ovals
under the ice.
She sees the heart
where all his shapes are known.

Spirit geometrizes in a lens of light
rainbowed between them.

A double pyramid at breast and thigh
the flesh stands bright as diamond and hard.

She touches him: he enters her,
their bodies leap like fishes in the net,
glister, go in and out,
dance their miraculous catch.

*

How should a corpse become a god
unless by contagion of pure gold
coined from the sun?

Let sheaves of gold fall on him like whale-brit.
Let him be littered in gold leaves;
diadems, amulets, pectorals, bracelets,
finger-stalls, sandals, necklaces, rings
tucked in each fold of the bandaging,
straps of gold leaf on his breast,
on his skull a great vulture in sheet gold
spreading its wings.

That his sight be made whole in the Afterworld,
as Isis now, Desdémona
offers for him her Litany of the Sun:

from the living darkness of an unhealed eye
behind the bandages

from the yellow spot in the marriage-chamber
of the visual purple

from the crocodile jealousy
which works to destroy what is perceived

by grace of the golden movement in the funeral dance
as a white bull between sycamores of turquoise

at the rising of his star pyramid in the Belt of Orion
he is redeemed.

And for that he she loved proved blind and did
forsake her,
now let him be changed into a beam of light.

*

Not more than twenty centimetres square,
a shaft of polished limestone open to the sky
and sloping down at forty-five degrees.
Half-way along, an alabaster door
worked like a portcullis from inside.

Isis grown adult in the brightest star
stands at her meridian.
Light floods the syrinx
palms the door
making a riffled backwash.

Inside the chamber
spirit-fingers grasp the copper handles.
The skyward shutter opens
and the star shines in.

On a couch of ebony
the body of a rag doll
and its little sister.
Plum-black unguent dries on them like jam.

The light informs itself into a silken bubble
and moves across the room.
A subtle envelope
it lingers in the air above their faces
and seems to breathe.
There is a music in its thousand angles.

It is not new.
These lachrimae
in the throat of the swallow
we have known before.
By a sycamore tree
or Babylon's fresh streams
snatches of old tunes.

The eyes of the foetuses unseel,
their limbs begin to stir.
Tears soften the stones,
make fibre-optic nerve-paths for the light.
The earthward corridor lies open.

A filmy breath, a breve,
blown from the aspiration of a sphere,
she spirit-levels down the syrinx
into the *Queen's Chamber* mis-named
where the blind one waits
embalmed and bound.

Sleive of the light
a gauzy spiralled wind-sock
floats in the room
seeking a face.

When the funeral masks are lifted one by one
the lips beneath are caulked with tar
and puckered like an amputation.
Not with an adze of meteorite
the opening of his mouth,
but with a slight insinuating tongue of air
quick as an asp.

There comes a whispered stranger in the throat.
Your veins are firm it says,
make love to me.

Priests touch the Osirian phallus with the adze,
star-sperm lasers the syrinx,
spirifers from the shaft
in a plume that seeds the sky.

In the hidden chamber
the twin unborn entwine.
Isis is got with child in the Milky Way,
Osiris lost in the Dog.
The swallows are the imperishable stars.

*

Love, what should I bring you
but new eyes
tied in a handkerchief.
Here are the knots of Isis.

These mirrors of rock-crystal
inlaid with amethyst,
their irises enlivened by a beam of light,
are miracles.
By these you shall perceive
all perfect, simple, calm and happy showings.

A hand may put out the candle
but memory
in the eye
lights it again.

My lord, I set you a task:
Describe in thy anatomy
what proportion exists
between the diameters
of all the lenses in the eye
and the distance from these
to the crystalline lens.

Love, we must study refraction.
You shall know me by the angle of the light.

I have not long.
The swallow's wing-tip
touches the sun's disc.
I steal the hours from paradise.

Look at me now.
Remember how we hunted the flamingo's smile?
Touch my cornelian.

Venus prospiciens
I am the goddess who looks out.

*

With a healed eye
by a just alignment
in the hidden chamber
at the fifth hour
the stars in their biding
restore the balance of the soul.

A feather tips the scales.

*

To see things differently,
to see things as they are
I had need of new eyesight.
She gave it. It belongs to her.
By grace of her own light
I see her now and all things differently.

In my solar barque
shaped like an open eye
I sail among constellations.
Flanked by images of yesterday
and tomorrow
between twin sentinels of fear
and gratitude
I navigate the circumpolar stars.
At the twelfth hour
my keel grazes the gold-capped apex
of the world-pyramid.
The earth is born
and time begins again.

There are histories, I learn,
where Cassio and Desdémona
a thousand times commit *the act of shame*
and unforbiddenly.
Or my lieutenant Iago
new-promoted
sleeps with me front-to-back
a very loving and an honest beast.
Possible worlds:
I know them and approve.
We learn to love unenviously here.

I threw away my world:
but *one entire and perfect chrysolite*
came back for me,
mended her unkind lord,
awoke my faith
and brought me here
to live among the gods.
I sing the music Desdemōna was.

The stars are sexual,
meteors our pheromones.
There are star children sometimes.
But here our love's magnetic
and non-degradable,
a distance
and a drawing.

Though sometimes she takes wing
a swallow under the sun
and nests in my sails,
such closeness is a grace conferred
and not of right.

Immutably related
we perish slowly and harmoniously
among the spheres.
We know the music that we make
does not depend on our existence.
Yet we must make it.

We cannot tell the mode of our projection.
The harpist of the seven vowels is blind.

An impassioned drawing
across a selfless distance,
the form precedes and beckons
and steals our life away.

*

Like fat kine in the green fields of Egypt
I give birth in tapestries of oxe-eye daisies,
my nightly wearing. Slippery as an eel
the boat of the soul shoots out between my thighs.
Full-breasted, Argus-eyed, I am star-stippled,
my milk goes everywhere, the Nile is white with it.
To the ends of the earth my arms reach down for him
and lift him by the hair, my man of gold.
Streaked with my blood and rainbowed like shot silk
I hold him close against my hollow womb.
Soul of the eve, soul of the morrow, my love
like the sun at the first waking of the world
with head of child and falcon wings is risen
from my nenuphar, from my blue lotus-flower.

*

8

Sati

Across the lake of tears
such filling light

scarlet-pated cranes
in a green quarantine
of distance

and cello
winding down
the stair of the *adagio*.

From here the mountain's shadow
will not reach the island.

The lake is a black mirror
its echo-surface hungry for a face.
Shade by shade it swallowed mine.

Lady of secret visions that refresh the eye,
do you hear the thunderous shelling
of love against the shore,
the symmetry of waves?

The god, like a pierced whale
bleeds without valve or stop
a constant flow.
His wound will heal
by being painful.
In that given world
radiancy streams from the eyes.
The inert stars absorb it
and grow bright.

On the crest of the mountain
a full moon
pure as the Host.

From a foreign land
a vision of white oxen
by the water's edge.

It is written
that on the day
and at the hour
of the rising of the Dog Star
the oryx raises a cry
and all the creatures
turning round
look to the east.

What are the eyes
with which Jokanaan
will perceive Salomé
at the end of the world?

The god of love a heap of ash.

Or to have seen that star.

II

Mene, mene . . .

When the ground floor went up in flames
the sound, in that muddy darkness
was ripped cardboard; the voices
like dogs shouting.
I thought: this is violent,
I'm definitely against it.
So I kept away,
watching them while they fired the block of flats.

When they saw me
some of them came across
and explained how it was difficult
setting light to curtains through broken windows,
because of the people inside the room
who lived there of course
and would do anything to prevent you.
They said you really had to keep trying with the flame
and use plenty of petrol, till at last it caught.

Then later, when it was mostly all over,
weaving between bodies of gypsy children
sleeping on the grass
she came skipping in turquoise and scarlet,
her bobbing black ponytail up at each step
like a carousel horse,
and grabbed hold of my arm.

They'd had to get out by the roof-hatches,
the men 'one metre apart' on the stairs
passing the children from hand to hand in the smoke.

'The disabled security man was a gon'er.
They knew which room he was in
but couldn't get through for the flames.
When we crawled over the tiles to the next block
none of the neighbours would take us.
No, they said. *Sorry. Our flat's too small*.
I'd honestly thought they'd be sympathetic,

but you're met with a mass indifference,
my mother says.

Last night some youngsters threw a woman from a train.
Her shopping first. Then, like more shopping, her.'

Between the sleeping children on the grass,
skipping in turquoise and scarlet; while at her back
these words were aerosol'd along the wall:
WHO SEEKS WILL FIND –
THE TRUTH LIES IN THIS TOWN.

The Child's Play of Antichrist

They'd given him a devout upbringing,
slaughter of chickens his higher education.
Evenings, while lamps were lit,
he'd be pushed down the back steps and left to get on with it.
Bolts clacked into place, and the hymn-singing began.

He could take his time,
no-one would come for him till dawn.
Claws tensed on their perches, the hens loosed a few droppings.
He let them settle down; cosied himself in the warm stink
snug as his own fart, or the smell of mother.

He had the saviour by the feet, tight in one fisted palm,
his thumb opposed on the loin-cloth.
Starting as he'd been taught, at the crown of thorns,
he signed himself with the five wounds.
Later, tasting fresh blood, he'd kiss them clean.

Always seven for the cull:
five for the table, one for the man of god
and the seventh his own, to toy with as he pleased
until three days were gone.
And then, the torture ending, killing came in again.

Striking out with the rood
he scythed a swathe from their roosts,
treading on some that fell,
while the rest ran squawking, like mothers raped of their children.
His free hand silenced the first throat.

They never died quickly.
He'd learned to feed on death-throes:
the feathered blood protesting, the insistent wings
from before Abraham was, his whole arm aching,
the thumb of the other hand choking the crucifix.

Some were swung by the feet,
their skulls cracked on the painted door-post.
Others beaten to death with the flat of the cross.
The cock bird, with ravaged comb,
impaled on the outstretched arms.

The seventh he took in both hands,
pinning its clipped wings;
let it struggle a while, then tucked it under his elbow
and stroked it from comb to tail with two fingers, forked.
Till it brooded at last, and he slept.

And the evening and morning were the first day.
In that snowfall waking, while his parents snored,
he went with the soldiers on the hill
stroking his pet, the way hands moved on the shine of the rifle,
their high-pitched song the crying of sea-birds, strangled.

They taught him the words
as carcases turned on a spit:
O beautiful foreign maiden, our monks will soon baptise you.
The warriors embrace you in the field of blackbirds.
Between their legs a crucifix converts your babies.

Dawn of the second day, broke a recurring dream
in which the hens were screwed
till they layed eggs with human faces.
Anguish tore him, as their smiles cracked wide
to hatch more chickens.

While the sun went down he toyed with the scared bird.
Then, at his mother's call, he set it free,
and the youths with cleavers chased it, till the head flew off
and the still running body
asperged the snow.

Early on the third day, the child still sleeping,
the cock bird rose from the heap of plucked carcases,
shivered its pinions in the sun, and with its beak
ripped out the golden corn from the split crops,
their breasts like pomegranates.

It stretched its neck
the nude flesh goose-pimpling, the comb inflamed,
and crowed in the ear of his dream *Rewind, rewind!*
His parents winged like harpies,
leaping from bed, falling on him, tearing.

Food for the gods:
a triptych from the Iliad

1

LOS MACHOS

The rabid scrimmage over dead Patróclus
under the walls of Troy;
husbands and fathers baying like famished dogs
for the scrag-end of a man.
Come on chaps!
Let's capture his corpse,
piss on it,
twist off the head
and kick for touch.
Loyally packed
as any from Wigan or St. Helen's,
classical types heave on their human hawser
till strands of his torso twist in the tugs of war.

There are so many ways to get glory.
A girl in someone's tent's turned inside-out for starters,
and left-overs will feed a thousand reputations.
You might pick up part of a head,
or hack off a cold foot;
something to prove your point
when you show the lads back home how with your spear
you gave the ultimate umpteenth jab
that fetched the living tripes of great Patróclus
all glistening from his side, like beans out of a can,
and so lay claim that it was you who killed him.

Hands at a table, scrabbling for dead flesh;
the officers' mess.

This camera-eye's as sharp as any Goya,
and always gets his picture, makes you look.
Two men engage.
One swings his blade,
lops off the other's head,

and while the stump still stands
we watch the moist pink marrow
well up from the vertebra,
protrude a bit,
congeal,
until the trunk keels over.

A boy of twelve
runs from the Trojan lines,
falls on his knees,
begs mercy of Achilles,
who strikes him in the liver with his sword,
laughing as the liver itself lolls out
purply into his lap,
velvet and wet,
for the boy to see it there:
himself, and edible.

O brave old world, that had such creatures in it.

The roots of our virility go far,
to find the parts philosophers can't reach.
What Plato ignored: enjoyment of the crunch
when the away boot stamps on the home face,
and vice-versa; the image of our future.

Yet Orwell only told the half of it.
That trodden face looks back
through an infinite regress of mutilation,
our fate to know no video nastier than history.

2

LA PENA

Only the orphaned horses weep sincerely,
there by the ships dismayed, mourning Patróclus,
scimitar-bladed necks curved to the sand,
their nostrils flared pink armholes, socks of flesh,
bellying the wind of grief.

Only a horse could weep sincerely,
only a river know to be appalled
when brave Greek men threw horses still alive
into the boiling rapids.

The wingless panic as he falls,
skull-smashing hooves flailing, dabbling the spray,
his rearing fuselage high as houses under the avalanche,
the limbs frantic, tangled in flying sheets; the cries
poured back down his throat.

Remorsefully, reluctantly, the river takes him.
The scarlet lungs waterlog, while the bronze flood
rolls his unbutchered carcase shamefully downstream,
bumping between rocks, catching in driftwood tangles,
until at last it bears him, by miles of estuarial sands,
stately as a tone-poem out to sea.

The tides refuse him many times;
and so by stages edge him sideways
into anonymous mud flats,
there to be sunk and stored.

3

FUNERAL GAMES

Six dukes stand by the long ships,
the yellow flamboys burning in their hands.

In Nestor's hall the girl Hecamedē
waits in the shadows:
two men tall by the door.

A hundred feet and then a hundred feet
the square is paced; the mourners pile the wood.

She moves the polished table into place,
her arms shine, lewed with torch-light.

Faces are wood, tears glisten there like sap,
while hands arrange his slack limbs for the fire.

She places a white onion in the dish;
beside it a mesh of brown honey, moist as lips;
tips from her hand soft meal of barley.

Cattle, wall-eyed, shamble towards the pole-axe,
sheep roll in the sand, matchstick legs pedal the air,
blades strip and scrape, the yellow fat is draped
over the body.

Her table is an altar, its enamelled legs
gleam like the thighs of Aztecs.
The lithe girl approaches, in her hands
the giant beaker, large as a pail.
Sets it. Round the base
eight feet in pairs make lions' paws,
from where four handles rise like cobras.
On their hoods
aurelian doves peck gold-dust.

Achilles leaps among the wild horses,
he runs for his dead friend, he is a wind,
his braking heel thumps the sand like a hoof.

Plunging through the surf of silver manes
he jerks a stallion by the cheek, and stabs it
from below. The beast rears, crazed.
Achilles soars with it, clinging to its neck,
then brings it down in a warm red flood.
Four great horses in this way he kills,
and crying for Patróclus,
drags their huge cadavers towards the pyre.

As she stoops over the great beaker
the girl's eyes mirror a gold iris.
She pours,
and a rippling pupil of magenta
swells to the shaded rim.
A bright meniscus tautens.
She blinks.
Darkling, her eyes are wine.

Achilles weeps, cuts the throats of his own dogs,
flings them at the pyre. Turns to the prisoners.
Chooses twelve.
Gripping his sword two-handed, faces the first.
Lowers the sharp point slowly.
Bows himself to the sand.
Tenses.
Rips once his arms to the sky,
shouts and unseams him.
Twelve times the simultaneous scream
swallows Achilles' cry.
Twelve times the voices eat each other.
Patróclus is enthroned on meat; the bodies lean like rifles.
Flesh, brick-red, sullenly oozes strenuous tears of blood.

She steadies the bronze grater; hands move;
a creamy snow lights on the surface of the wine.
Her smile beckons; she sprinkles barley;
a yeast of bubbles gathers at the brim.
Behind her, Titian shadows loom, the dark is warm.
Flames glint in the shine of the cup, in the men's eyes.
Light salivates the rounded lips, brushes the fingertips,
as Nestor drinks.

Wine stains the sand.
Patróclus clutches a sprig of Achilles' hair
placed in his hands.
A breeze beats up the sallow flame
that stutters in the green wood.
The lion fire roars in the sky all night.
In the yellow light
a man crawls,
pouring from a golden cup, groaning,
trawling a purple shadow in the sand.

The great cup is empty.
Nestor sleeps.
The girl has gone.

With sparkling wine put out the fire, and cool the crimson ash.
Under the failing stars take up the bones, but only his,
and lay them in a golden vase.
Close up the mouth with double seals of lard,
and take it to his hut.
Wrap it in linen.
Then go and build his grave.

An invasion of privacy

There's a poem I have to write that won't come off.
My brain feels like a blanket,
imagination sticks to it like – faugh!
Worse than TV, where Thames's muddy flow
keeps Coleridge's birthday.
From the South Bank the voices come and go,
talking of pleasure-domes.
I fall asleep – at least, I think I do –
and then the dreams begin.

Arm-flailing stiffs without seat-belts
three bodies fling out from a doorway,
and far too deeply involved, a dark fourth
mixed up with them writhes like a bruised eel.
They hitch him about on the ground obscenely,
till one from below somehow rolls him up onto his feet,
then lissom, leaps with him into the air,
curls over, and dolphin on dolphin falling
smashes face into concrete.

I'm out of it over the road, and children are there.
Here's sunshine strangely, the spaced-out air
gives a sense of the seaside; but eyes stay skinned
to the small-screen drama unfolding
in that contracted courtyard, where fall-out
of grained twilight invests the scuffed clothes,
the industrial brick of the buildings
between which they slither him under a wall
and a drain-pipe serves to prop him against
while one of them's beer sick.

Then they go for it: bunched fists to the groin,
off-hand karate-chops aimed at pressure-points
not quite in focus; like drunken soldiers
hammering-in nails. Why couldn't I move?
I should have gone in like Antigonē,
dragged off the dead.

No need to ask where it comes from, all this.
The sacred river's poisoned; effluent's got into the Id.
Persons on porno-business dish our dreams.
Someone stuck this video in, it won't eject.
Unbid, the visible worm winds in my head.

Punctum

Kirkup, on Radio,
speaks of places in Japan
where, in the public parks
at the height of summer,
ghost-plays are performed
to chill the spine.

And somewhere, he says,
a shrine has been built
where crowds gather
to offer up prayers
for the life-after-death
of a thousand used bra's.

Here in my English orchard
handfuls of haemoglobin
stripped from the redcurrant
spill like Grandmother's beads,
and my four guinea-fowl
seem to be wearing her dress.

The shells of their pear-shaped eggs
are the almost brown
of your breasts in summer,
and faintly stippled.
Three cracked in the pan
make a good frying, their yolks

bright as the bills of my three white geese.
I shall print my happiness white
on the white sheet.
The milk of your breast
leaves no mark
on the milk-white cup.

Today it's too hot to write,
but on small-screen, late-night,
we watch the end of empire.

Where Baltic pack-ice melts in blood,
Latvia, Estonia, float free:
theatre to chill the spine.

In Lithuania, a hill of crosses.
Levelled each year,
they spring like grass again,
the distant decomposed
brought back,
re-buried.

On the fragile green breast of Siberia
a man is seeking his mother.
They open the grave,
and her face, still on the skull,
smiles at him sadly; sags
in its make-up of silvery mud.

We all re-bury our mothers.
Mine from the spoil-heaps of Wincobank
gently uplifted, in May-time,
the headstone subsiding,
my writing no use to her now,
all to do still.

Ghost-plays in the heat of summer.
Like the actor in Kabuki
who takes the Woman's part,
I should black my teeth
and when I laugh,
flash a dark crescent.

Closure

October: time of turning leaves.
Our fast train to London dives
through a gorge lined thick with them,
aiming at Westminster.
They panic in our on-rush,
the tawny yellows, the startled sallows,
make car-wash at our windows.
We're riding our own wake for once,
caught in a sleeve of autumn
that's pulling inside-out.

Our hopes rush on towards Parliament,
but a million words too many
bleed on the floor
of that abattoir.
No-one believes, or is believed.
We're side-tracked to Hyde Park.
Trees cast a few votes,
and we walk with the miners there,
shuffling between police,
a few too many, treading the leaves.

It's Fall; the jobs rain down in shoals.
Money shifts under the house like sand.
Past the church of the Carmelite friars
we march with the twice defeated.
And still that flamey light comes off them.
Sales-girls out from the posh shops
let it lick at them, flirt with it a bit.
Give o'er that! comes from behind,
Tha's married. All he'd done was smile.
No toe-jobs for madonnas here.

Back-end: the year's recessional and ours.
The pound must find its floor.
Colliery brass bands
rock-a-bye leaves from the boughs
with some old tunes from Hadēs.

Stung by the price of a lemonade,
I'll tell thee what, says one,
we s'll not be coomin 'ere
to do us shoppin! They'll hardly win.
But the firecoals of their voices, going down.

Exequy
in memoriam Olivier Messiaen

All that last winter, on through aching spring
and deep into the moonstruck harvest,
nothing had felt so good as lying down,

dressed in his dayclothes, with his slippers on,
and not to sleep – or hardly – just to lie,
a silent, stone-carved emblem of himself.

With eyelids closed, in darkness like the mole,
limbs drugged by cessation, entropy pulling down
the sides of the mouth and straightening out the feet,

he's taken leave of his senses – all but one –
left them on pilot-light, a corposant
of still blue flames that purr inside his head.

Each day, become his own sarcophagus,
he sepultures himself, draws down the lid,
and feeds on rich chromatic dark behind the eyes.

Pale laser hands move blindfold through the brain,
carving his shape from silence like cut breath.
Loose as all water, gravid as sculpted stone,

like Chaucer's *smale foweles* in *Aprille,*
he sleeps with one sense posted; not the eye,
but lives in the waking ear, with parted lips.

The gates of the labyrinth stand open.
Music strikes. Ichor of birdsong,
joie du sang des étoiles, runs in his veins.

*

Until we dead awaken. Side by side
in this cool greenstone chamber of the wall,
our effigies pick up the swell of plainchant.

Entombed as in a bath of sound, we may not look
or speak; our fingers barely touch.
The singing has rinsed out all other sense.

Yet once in a thousand years bestir, bestir.
Blood stipple the sandstone in a Chinese burn.
Cover me with your shadow; slip your tongue
a clove between my lips. Let the stone taste.

In waterlight

1

When the blown glass in crisis
viscid and molten still
suffered the pang of cooling

she felt the sky
arc over her
so charged a sapphire

the wave's deep aquamarine
rose up in her
to meet it.

2

Her eyes were chrysoprase
of the rain-light walking the water
where islands kneel to mountains
in sound of Raasay.

And hers the one face ever.

Earth and sky at two backs
they made the beast of love
in the hot grass.

When their bodies answered
he felt the sun stoop:
and saw in the grey-green iris
a bird fly over the sea
behind his head.

3

Melt-water
bled from the mountain
to the fall at Lympa.

I walked into the pool
and you flowed round me
like a second skin

seizing my heart in ice
your element
and mirror of the soul.

Morning and night
it bleeds pure water now
for you to wash in.

Clean, warm,
closer than hands
it maps your skin with rivers.

Our year comes by.
The pool is full again:
unclothe.

Brother Ass

Snow fell on Mount La Verna;
winter frit the branches,
miracled the waterfall
to bone of ice.

No fire in the cave
where Francis prays.
And yet he burns.
Paul had been right:
better to marry than this.

The hidden paparazzo,
with zoom lens cocked for stigmata,
tells how the saint
rushed out from the cave
stripped off his clothes
gathered up armfuls of snow,
and in his frenzy
built for himself
not snow-men,
but shapes of naked women
nubile and smooth,
and threw himself upon them
crying *This is my wife!*
This is my lover!
This is my paramour!

Today, a beaded frost is rimed
on grass-blade, fence-post, twig;
a close-up photo-film in black and white
(but mostly white) of someone's skin:
as though the instant sweat, the lew
that Marilyn distilled for camera-men
simply by thinking so,
had fallen in the night
and covered everything.

Since you're away,
I rush out in the cold –

Maggiolaté:
songs for the five senses, in Leonardo's notation

1

Oh too far off by far – but listen, listen.
Do you hear the capillaries' in-
consolable bleeding; how the flesh weeps,
and the birds' singing a nest of thorns
between us?

There is a scale of journeys, music
of separations: you diminished
at each milepost to a third, a fourth,
a perfect fifth; Pythagoras' comma
fading out the octave.

Why should the cuckoo lay her eggs astray?
Her song's an echo, harking for what's gone.
True summer's always somewhere else.
Meantime our spring: a gargling of grains of gold
in the starling's throat.

2

Disturbed by blowing of winds,
what sifting of watery humours in the lion's nose?
It is her mate; she tells him from far off.
The kill hangs in his jaws like a mantle.

Or what shall be said of the musk?
I smell your skin; you might as well be here.
Apple-scent, dew-fall of blossom, a throat of glass,
and cinnamon a yellow stain upon the lozenge.

3

When we burnished our throats with the Calvados, mouth to mouth,
and our tongues in flame described the seven principal movements,

were we not raised to a power of infinite points of light?

What the soul longs to taste is the mouth.
When you speak to me gently, I will note your lips.

4

We lie in the one flesh like water,
our hands swim in and out
in forty demonstrations.

Pressed between us, interleaved,
without centre or boundary
nothingness spreads its limbs.

Our souls cast a single shadow.
I am changed:
you moved.

5

After surprising rain
the sky is a crystalline lens
and the sun *a nerve bored through*
to that world of light.

Up high
cirrus slips against stratus
in flimsy underskirts.
Our green Earth is abashed.

Between the trees
(your delicate clown)
the swallow, with his net of mirrors,
baffles the air with images of you.

Mathematical flowers,
they pass through one another
without confusion,
continuous, yet distinct.

DONALD ATKINSON's first collection, *A Sleep of Drowned Fathers*, published by Peterloo Poets in 1989, won the Aldeburgh Poetry Festival Prize of the following year, for the best first collection of the previous twelve months. His second volume, *Graffiti for Hard Hearts*, was published by Littlewood Arc (now Arc Publications).

Writing in the magazine *Ambit,* Peter Porter describes the first book as "a triumph of storytelling, a vindication of the sanguine view that poetry can handle terrible themes with as much directness and realism as prose". He goes on to say: "With *Graffiti*, Donald Atkinson joins the company of accomplished masters among contemporary poets. His writing is always beautiful. In the end though, it is the intensity of the writing which commands respect, its uncompromising view of life."

Donald Atkinson won First Prize in both the Peterloo Poets Open Competition and the TLS Cheltenham Festival Competition of 1988, and his work has appeared in the *Blue Nose Anthology* of 1993, the *Forward Anthology* of 1994 and the British Council's *New Writing 5*. In 1995, he received a Writer's Award from the Arts Council of England.

Originally from Yorkshire, of partly Scottish ancestry, he now lives in Saffron Walden..